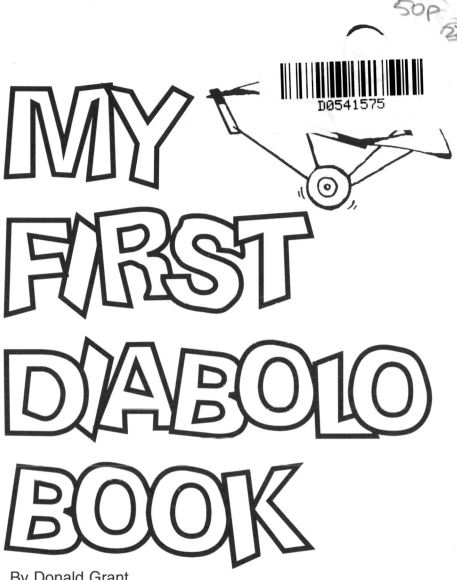

MY FIRST DIABOLO BOOK

By Donald Grant

Illustrated by Donald Grant
Produced and Published by CIRCUSTUFF

Copyright © 1995

ISBN 0 9520300 5 5

First published 1995
Reprinted 1998, 2001

ISBN 0 9520300 5 5

Published by
CIRCUSTUFF
83 Uist Rd
Pitcoudie
Glenrothes
Fife
KY7 6RE
United Kingdom

http://www.circustuff.com/

Other CIRCUSTUFF Titles

By Donald Grant:

"Diabolo Stick Grinds and Suicides"
"Diabolo 2: Crazy Cradles and Baffling Body Moves"
"Diabolo 3: Two Hot to Handle" (with added Guy Heathcote)
"Totally Diabolical"

Shaun Clark's "Cigar Box of Tricks"

"The Book of Club Swinging" by Ben Richter

"Stunning Starts and Fancy Finishes for Club Jugglers" by Doug
Dougal

"Mastering Devilstick (part one)" by Chris Dore

"Take 3 Clubs" by Robert Dawson

Contents

INTRODUCTION

Welcome to the dastardly domain of the diabolo! If you've just picked up (or even, heaven forbid, bought) this book, then it's reasonably safe to assume that you are just starting out. Lucky old you: although the prop itself has been around for centuries, there has never been a better time to get into it!

Originally from China (and made out of bamboo), it has enjoyed brief surges of popularity throughout the ages. Indeed, between 1907 and 1908 it became a full-blown craze amongst both child and adult alike, long before other widgets such as hula-hoops and yo-yos had their day. But now, with the sudden surge of public interest in all sorts of juggling, the diabolo is enjoying a big comeback. There are many new performers, new precision-made smooth spinning diabolos and a whole array of new tricks (even involving more than one diabolo at once, skills which the Chinese themselves had once believed impossible!)

With a bit of luck, this book will guide you through getting started and the first twenty-odd tricks. Read carefully, stay relaxed, and the learning process shouldn't be too painful. Practice is essential, but if you get bogged down or frustrated, remember you can just walk away and come back to it later (I know, I know, it isn't easy!)

So what are you waiting for? Grab your diabolo, turn the page and enter the wonderful world of high throws, tangled string and spindescribable mayhem!

Have fun!

Donald Grant

ANATOMY OF THE PROP

Just in case you don't know, this is what a diabolo looks like. Don't let the sophisticated terminology confuse you ...

STRING LENGTH
A point of considerable debate, this. Generally speaking, with one handstick flat on the floor, the string should usually come up to anywhere between chest and eye level.

Longer strings make for easier cat's cradles, more impressive "round the worlds" and are a bit easier for learning two diabolos on.

Shorter strings are better for faster routines and also for learning many of the more difficult two diabolo tricks.

In the long run, it all comes down to your height and personal choice. Experiment and see which you prefer.

HOW TO START

Okay, now pay attention. As you may gather, this is the most important piece of information in the whole book!

These instructions assume you are right handed. If you're not, I'm sure you're very experienced at reversing all right and left hand references.

1) Start with the diabolo on the floor to your right hand side.

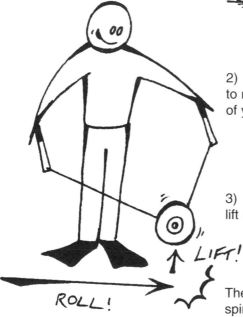

2) Use the handsticks and string to roll it along the ground in front of you to the left.

3) Once it passes your left foot, lift up the handsticks to pick it up.

The diabolo should now be spinning.

4) As soon as you lift the diabolo from the ground, make regular short upwards movements with your *right hand only* to keep it spinning.

Allow your left hand to move only slightly, pulled down by the power stroke of your right hand, then springing back to its start position.

NB The movement is not evenly balanced - if you pull up with your left hand you will slow the diabolo down!

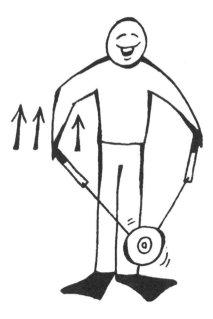

There you go. That wasn't too painful after all, was it?

CONTROL

Now that you've got the little rascal spinning, you'll find that it occasionally tilts off centre. Never fear, the cure is safe at hand: pay attention, because it is very simple.

If the diabolo tilts towards you, then push away with your right hand - the power stroke.

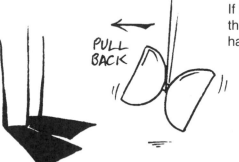

If the diabolo tilts away from you, then pull back with your right hand.

And that's all there is to it:
Your left hand does nothing.
Your right hand does it all.

HOW TO TURN

Right, so now you can control your diabolo, you might as well learn how to turn it as well.

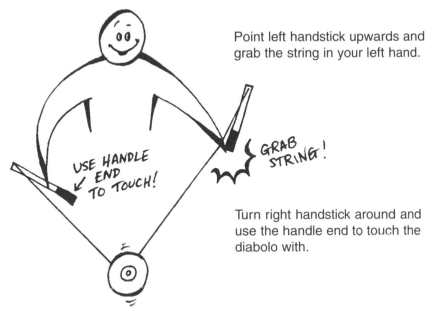

Point left handstick upwards and grab the string in your left hand.

Turn right handstick around and use the handle end to touch the diabolo with.

Touching at the 12 o'clock point on the inside rim of the cups will turn the diabolo in the following directions:

Near side cup = clockwise turn.
Far side cup = anticlockwise turn.

Very useful if you have to chase your audience through twisting streets.

THROW AND CATCH

Boy oh boy! Are you lucky or what? It just so happens that the first trick you learn is also one of the most impressive in the whole book. It doesn't matter how many tricks you go on to learn, every now and again nothing feels better than simply throwing the diabolo high into the air and catching it again. Audiences seem to enjoy it too!

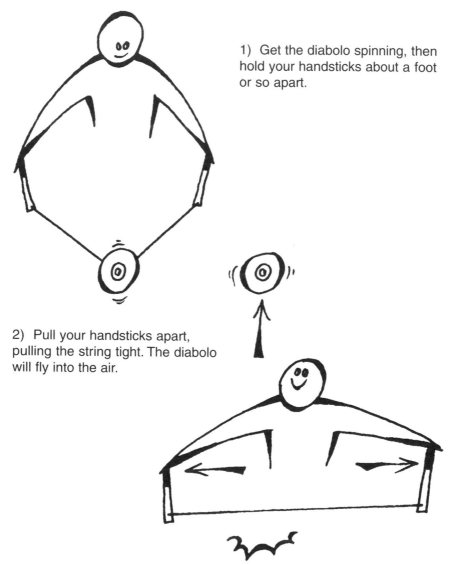

1) Get the diabolo spinning, then hold your handsticks about a foot or so apart.

2) Pull your handsticks apart, pulling the string tight. The diabolo will fly into the air.

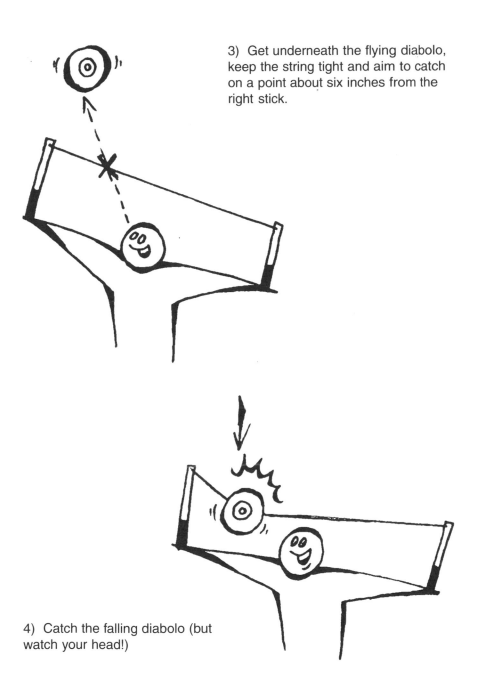

3) Get underneath the flying diabolo, keep the string tight and aim to catch on a point about six inches from the right stick.

4) Catch the falling diabolo (but watch your head!)

13

5) Bring your handsticks together to absorb the impact.

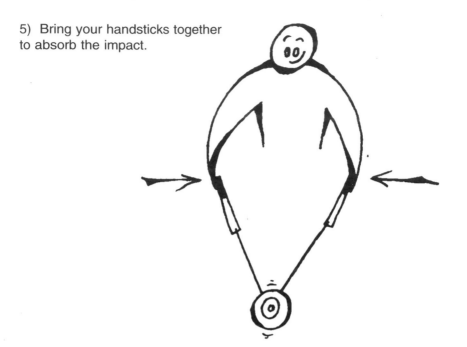

The throw must go above head height so that you get a chance to "aim" your catch, but apart from that, "the sky's the limit" generally.

Please be careful of low ceilings, high winds, power lines, trees, birds, aeroplanes, super heroes and such like ...

WHIPPING

Many of the tricks in this book require the diabolo to be spinning at relatively high speeds. This, as you have probably discovered, can take some time using the regular old driving method. The technique of whipping, therefore, may be just what you've been praying for. The action is fairly simple.

1) Pull to the right with the right handstick.

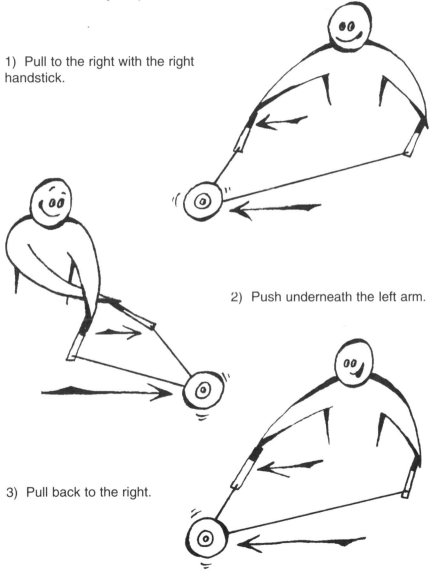

2) Push underneath the left arm.

3) Pull back to the right.

Three or four well-timed "whips" should be enough to get your diabolo spinning well. The only problem with this is that you will now find that your diabolo has tilted off centre.

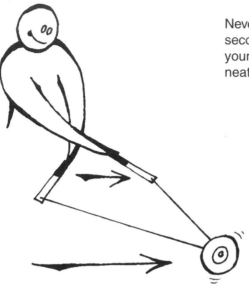

Never fear. To cure this, on every second whip, push over the top of your left arm instead of underneath.

Thus the complete whipping sequence should look like this:
pull to right - push under left - pull to right - push over left etc etc.

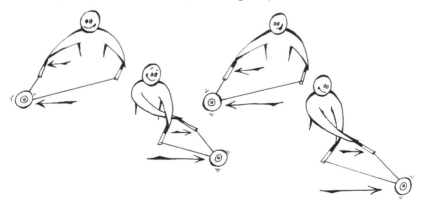

This action does take quite a bit of practice to get smooth, but it is 100% essential that you learn it. (To an audience, the rapid side to side movement of the diabolo is quite impressive too!)

FOOT HOP

Here you go: your very first body move. This is the first time you've incorporated part of your anatomy into the middle of a trick.

It probably won't be the last.

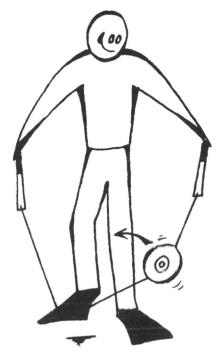

1) Get the diabolo spinning low on the left side. Place your foot against approximately the mid-point of the string.

2) Pull up with your left hand to tighten the string against your foot and hop the diabolo over.

And you thought your feet were just there for decoration, didn't you?

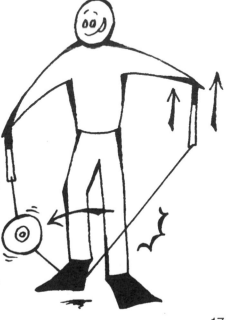

AROUND THE LEG

This is the grown-up version of the previous trick. It's a little harder to master but far more elegant once you've put in a bit of practice.

1) Have the diabolo slightly to the left side of the string and insert the leg of your choice.

2) Pop the diabolo over your leg, then let it pass back under.

At first you can perform this trick standing on one leg, but eventually you should be able to do it continuously with both feet firmly on the floor.

STRING CLIMB

This move has it all! It's mysterious, visually impressive and a guaranteed crowd pleaser. Best of all it isn't all that difficult to learn. All you need is a *very* fast spinning diabolo and the following instructions ...

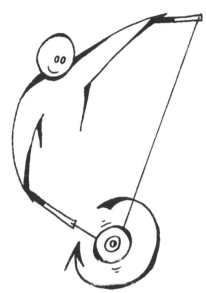

1) Get the diabolo spinning about 4 or 5 inches from the right handstick. Hold the left handstick up high.

2) Using the right handstick, loop the string around the axle with a circular gesture around the far side cup of the diabolo.

PULL TIGHT!

3) Pull the string tight. The diabolo will climb the string!

ASTONISHING!

4) When it gets to the top, unloop the axle with a circular motion of the left handstick around the near side cup.

Now mop your brow and take that stunned expression off your face. I told you it would work. Oh ye of little faith ...

SKIP THE STRING

If you can do a high throw, and
your feet haven't been mysteriously nailed to the floor, you can
do this trick.

1) Throw the diabolo up in the air
(watch where it's going!)

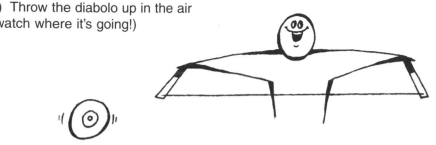

MIGHTY
LEAP!

2) As the diabolo peaks, take a
mighty leap over the string.

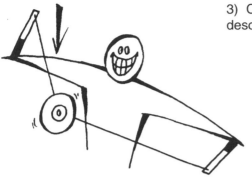

3) Catch the diabolo as it descends.

For the truly athletic amongst you, you can also try:

Two skips: This is easier the "Chinese" way, where you skip using alternate steps (eg first skip left step, second skip right step) rather than taking two mighty two-footed leaps.

Double skip: Whereby the string swings *twice* in one leap. It's probably best to practice this one without the diabolo at first.

PIROUETTE

Again, this trick shouldn't present any real problems, so long as you can already perform a high throw.

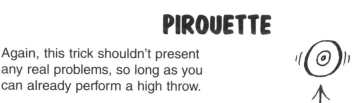

1) Pop the diabolo into the air, taking note of where it's heading.

2) When it peaks, pull your arms in and pirouette quickly.

3) Spot the diabolo and catch it as it descends.

Whatever you do:
Don't try to pirouette until the diabolo is thrown.
Don't try to watch the diabolo as you pirouette.

Although double pirouettes are possible, it's usually more fun to see how low you can do them. Just above head height is impressive. Shoulder height is brilliant. Waist height qualifies you for instant deification.

22

AROUND THE ARM

The most important thing about this move is to ensure that your arm is in the correct position, otherwise you will only make things harder than they need be.

1) Assume the position:
Upper arm parallel with the floor.
Forearm vertical.
Wrist cocked.

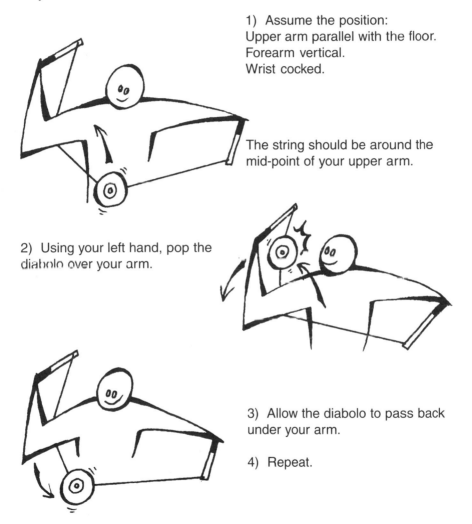

The string should be around the mid-point of your upper arm.

2) Using your left hand, pop the diabolo over your arm.

3) Allow the diabolo to pass back under your arm.

4) Repeat.

Although it is more than likely that you will develop a favourite arm, make sure that you learn *and* practice this move on *both* sides. You'll see why when you progress to some of the more advanced body moves.

NECK BOUNCES

Audiences seem to like it when you perform this trick. Maybe it's because it is visually impressive. Maybe it's because it looks like there's a real chance that you might choke yourself. I prefer to try not to think about such things.

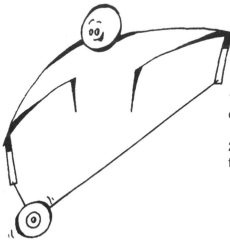

1) Get your diabolo spinning close to your right handstick.

2) Turn 90 degrees to look along the string at the diabolo.

3) Loop the string around the back of your neck using your left handstick.

4) Ensuring that the string is of equal length on both sides, hop the diabolo back and forth between them.

To escape from this position simply reverse the steps. And just in case you get complacent, why not try pirouetting in between the occasional bounce???

UNWRAP AND RECAPTURE

This move may appear simple and unimpressive, but it is absolutely essential to any of the more advanced moves which you will learn later on. It also helps you to get used to the idea of having your arms or strings crossed.

1) Pop the diabolo up on the right hand side (no more than a foot).

2) Bring the right handstick around and over the top of the diabolo, so that the "underside" of the string catches on the top of the axle.

3) Move the right handstick under the diabolo and cross your arms left over right.

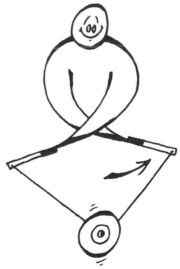

4) Throw to escape.

All of this should occur as one smooth motion. It is not easy at first, but perseverance will pay off. If you have any trouble, get someone else to hold the diabolo still while you go through the move.

And just as you seem to be getting the hang of it, you suddenly realise that you are going to have to switch the instructions around in order to learn it on the left hand side too. It's just not fair, is it?

ROUND THE WORLD MK 1

The first of many tricks which comes under the collective title of "round the worlds". This is the easiest of them all and should get you used to the sensation of swinging the diabolo. As with all round the world tricks, a decent amount of spin is recommended before you start.

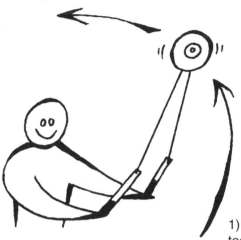

1) Keeping your wrists fairly close together, swing the diabolo to your left in a big circle.

2) As it completes the circle, you will see that the string is twisted.

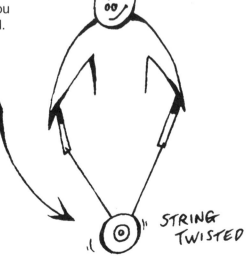

STRING TWISTED

3) To remove the twist, simply swing the diabolo in another circle, this time to the right.

4) If everything seems to work, then congratulations! You may proceed to the Mk 2 version.

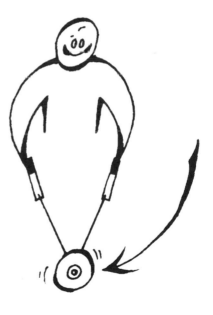

ROUND THE WORLD MK 2

A much nicer variation than the "Mk 1", as it avoids any twisting of the string. It is however, as you are about to find out, a teensy weensy bit dangerous.

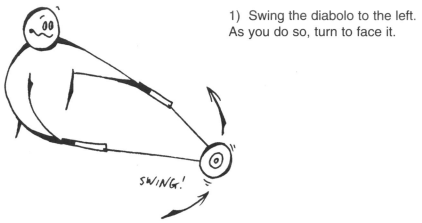

1) Swing the diabolo to the left. As you do so, turn to face it.

SWING!

2) Allow the diabolo to swing round, passing *between your arms*.

NB If the diabolo doesn't pass cleanly between both your arms, then you'll end up with a loop or a twist in the string.

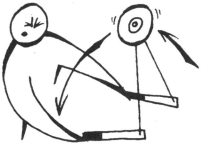

PHEW!

This trick can be performed with swings to both left and right, and also with both clockwise *and* anti-clockwise swings.

Learn them all, but please be careful. If you have a long string, it is possible to strike yourself with the diabolo on various parts of your anatomy
(the least painful of which is your chin!)

ROUND THE WORLD PIROUETTE

A very elegant round the world
trick is usually best performed
slowly and gracefully.

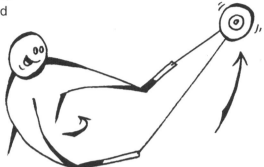

1) Swing the diabolo firmly
to your left. Keep your
hands no more than about
a foot apart.

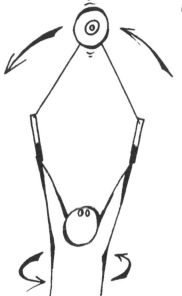

2) As the diabolo reaches about
two o'clock, start the pirouette.

3) By twelve o'clock, you should
be half way through the pirouette
Keep your eyes on that diabolo.
And keep going.

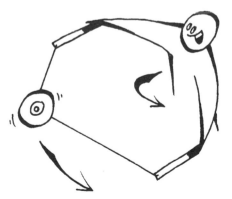

4) As you finish the pirouette, the
diabolo should complete its swing
to finish in front of you, string
untwisted.

The secret of this trick is not to rush it; swing the diabolo firmly, then
simply follow it round. Even the most lumbering of clods can be made to
look dainty with this trick, honestly.

29

FIGURE 8 ROUND THE WORLD

Technically, this is no more difficult than two consecutive round the worlds, but the visual effect is far more striking.

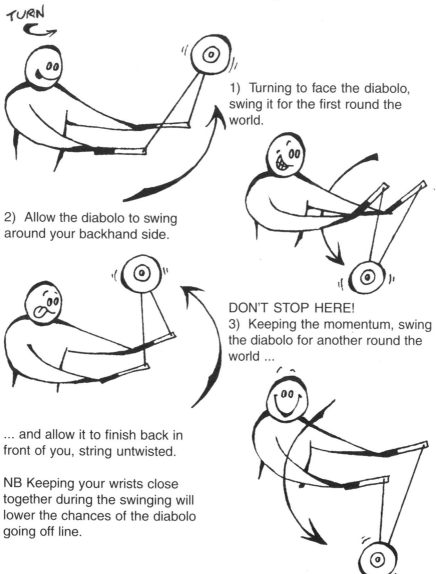

TURN

1) Turning to face the diabolo, swing it for the first round the world.

2) Allow the diabolo to swing around your backhand side.

DON'T STOP HERE!
3) Keeping the momentum, swing the diabolo for another round the world ...

... and allow it to finish back in front of you, string untwisted.

NB Keeping your wrists close together during the swinging will lower the chances of the diabolo going off line.

This trick is a valuable element for round the world sequences and should really be learned on both sides for the sake of symmetry.

ROUND THE WORLD STOPOVER

Yet another round the world variation to test your skill ...

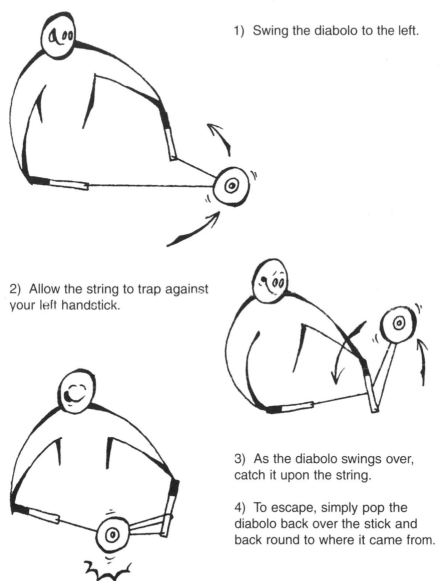

1) Swing the diabolo to the left.

2) Allow the string to trap against your left handstick.

3) As the diabolo swings over, catch it upon the string.

4) To escape, simply pop the diabolo back over the stick and back round to where it came from.

It looks nice if you perform this move first on one side, then on the other, just in case you're interested.

DOUBLE STOPOVER

Ooh! The big brother of the previous trick. You'll need a long string and a lot of spin for this one.

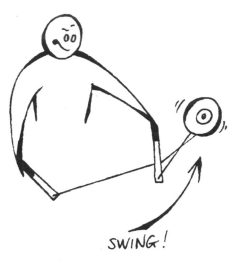

SWING!

1) Swing a stopover on the left.

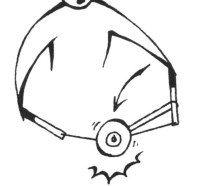

2) Now swing *another* stopover, this time to the right.

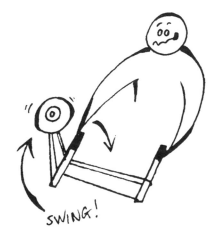

SWING!

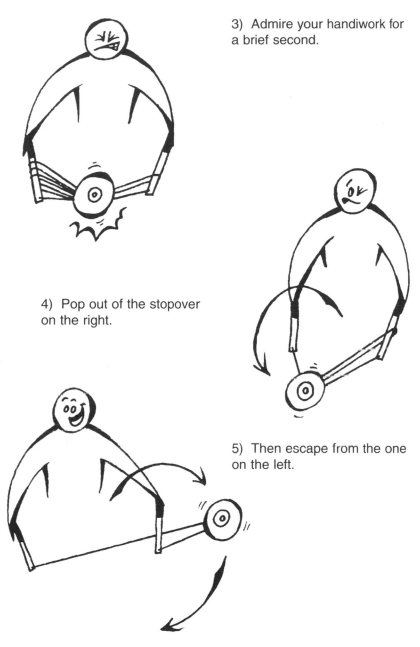

3) Admire your handiwork for a brief second.

4) Pop out of the stopover on the right.

5) Then escape from the one on the left.

This trick is complicated enough to impress most cynics, but only if you manage to escape from it whilst still spinning. So make sure you give it a good dose of whipping before you go for it.

ARM SCOOP MK 1

This is the first of two "arm scoop" tricks, all of which look best when incorporated into a sequence of moves around the arm.

1) From around the right arm, bring the right hand down and under the diabolo so the string passes beneath it.

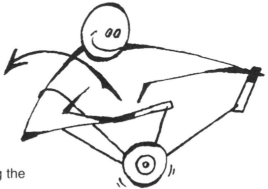

2) Scoop upwards, lifting the diabolo up over your arm.

3) Allow your wrist to break so that diabolo swings around to in front of you.

4) Your arms/string should now be crossed, right over left. Throw to escape.

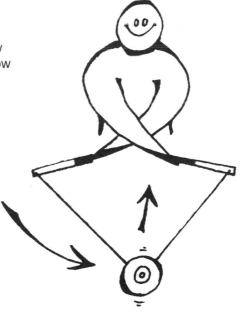

And if that one was too easy, wait until you see the next one ...

ARM SCOOP MK 2

Slightly harder this one: follow the instructions carefully, *especially* the finishing position, to avoid getting in a tangle.

1) From around the right arm position, pop the diabolo up 2 or 3 inches ...

... and bring the left handstick underneath, then over the top of it.

SCOOP DOWN!

2) Scoop down on top of the diabolo.

3) Allow it to swing down and around the right arm.

4) As the diabolo comes over the top of your right arm, bring your left arm across your body.

The diabolo should finish sitting in a small cradle over your right arm.

5) Throw to escape.

THROW

All this should happen as one smooth action. If you have any trouble, get someone else to hold the diabolo for you as you go through the move slowly.

CAT'S CRADLE MK 1

This is the easiest of all cat's cradle moves as the diabolo never leaves the string at any point.

1) After generating a moderate amount of spin, point your hand-sticks towards one another and move them together, one above the other.

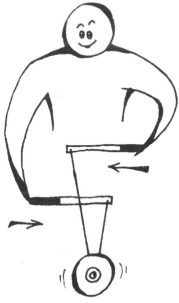

2) By "pedalling" one handstick over the other you should reach this position.

3) "Pedal" again and the diabolo should sit in the small window in the middle of the cradle.

4) To escape, simply perform the manoeuvre in reverse.

Although this is a fairly simple "no risk of dropping" move, if you perform it quickly in the middle of a routine your audience will more often than not become pleasantly baffled.

CAT'S CRADLE MK 2

Although significantly more difficult than the other cat's cradle, the end product isn't really any more impressive. In fact, your audience may find the intricate weaving more entertaining than the final product.

Such is life: take the adulation where you can get it !

1) Perform an "unwrap and recapture" so you end up with your arms crossed.

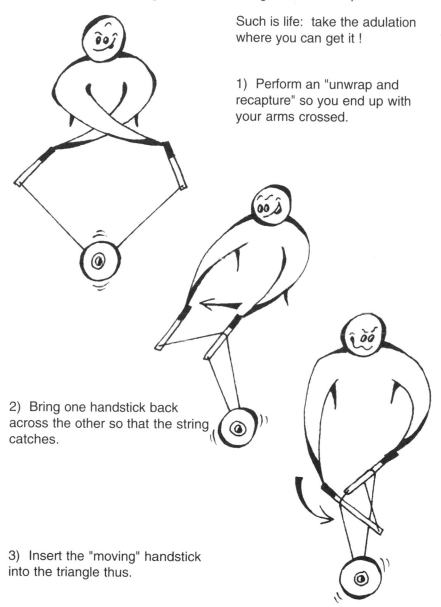

2) Bring one handstick back across the other so that the string catches.

3) Insert the "moving" handstick into the triangle thus.

4) Pull tight and erect your handsticks to form something like this.

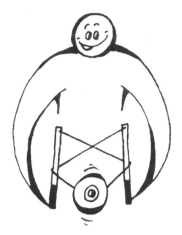

5) Ping the diabolo high into the air ...

... and catch it on top of the cradle.

To escape from this position, simply tip your handsticks downwards so that the string slides off, mysteriously untangled and with the diabolo still spinning upon it. Spooky eh ?

STICK GRINDS

A "stick grind" is any trick where the diabolo spins (or "grinds") against the handstick. Many disregard grinds as an unimpressive throwaway trick. Hopefully I can convince you otherwise ...

I describe grinds using the following terms:

"OUTWARD" GRIND.

Outward grind, where the diabolo is spinning away from the hand. It lasts longer than and is slightly easier than the ...

Inward grind, where the diabolo is spinning towards the hand. Both should be learned (on both left and right sticks) to ensure success in some of these tricks.

"INWARD" GRIND.

A fair measure of spin is also necessary for most grinds, so a good dose of whipping will be required before attempting each move.

Here are several handy hints guaranteed to help your diabolo grind further:

Rubbing small amounts of wax into your handsticks.
Using handsticks made from aluminium or fibreglass.
Spray painting or laquering your sticks (nicer looking too !)
Using a diabolo with a one piece axle.

By employing one or more of these aids you can ensure a much smoother and (almost) endless spin upon your handsticks.

So don't just sit there: wax up and get grinding !

EASY STICK GRIND

This is the first - and sometimes the only - stick grind trick that people learn. it provides essential practice for getting used to the sensation of grinding.

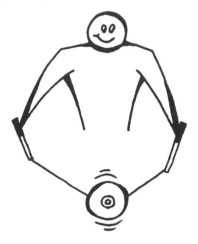

The trick itself is very simple:

1) Raise one handstick while holding the other at the correct angle (depending on whether the diabolo is spinning "inward" or "outward").

2) Allow the diabolo to slip onto the lower stick and grind there for a moment.

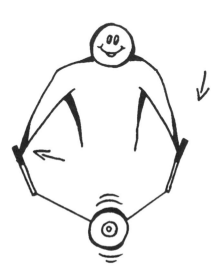

3) Let the diabolo slip back onto the string.

Practice both inward and outward grinds on both right and left sticks as you will need them for more complex grinds!

SUICIDE ATTEMPT

This is the basic suicide upon which other moves are based. So practice this one to death before attempting any others, and you should do just fine.

Relax. Take a breath. There's a first time for everything and this is probably the first trick where you've let go of the handstick deliberately. Don't panic, it's not as hard as it looks.

1) Swing the diabolo as if you're doing "around the world" to the left.

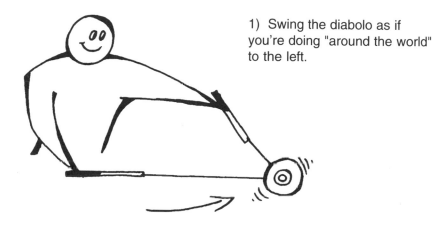

2) As the diabolo reaches a 12 o'clock position, let go of the right handstick.

RELEASE

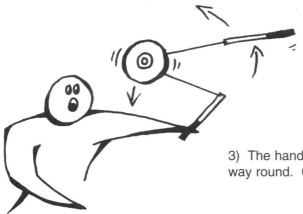

3) The handstick will swing all the way round. Catch it !

Catching the handstick relies upon 10% skill and 90% faith. Trust me: the trick does work.

CATCH!

Your first suicides will be huge, wild, swooping affairs.

But with practice, it is possible to control their size by making a small circular gesture with the "held" handstick after you've released the other.

The only other advice I can give is practice, practice and keep practicing.

THE LAST WORD...

So you've reached the end book. So you've managed to learn all the tricks? You haven't?!! Never mind, I won't tell anyone ...

By now you've probably realised just how versatile a prop the diabolo is. If you're interested, there are other books in this series, all containing harder, flashier and stranger tricks than you ever dared dream of. Not that this is some cheap advertising scam or anything!

Don't forget to use your imagination, however. With a bit of application, you can often come up with new tricks and variations of your own. Remember: books like this should be treated as guides, not encyclopaedias!

Take care and keep whipping!

PS Thanks and greetings to the following helpers, friends and performers: Stewart Hutton, Pearse, Guy, Brendan, Bruce, Ewan, Dave and anyone else I've forgotten.

Further diabolical reading matter from Donald Grant ...

ISBN 0 9520300 0 4
48 pages, 94 line illus, P/back
"Donald has taken two basic tricks and explored their full potential ... in a nice relaxed style with great illustrations." The Catch. "Engaging style ... clear and charmingly illustrated." Juggler's World.

ISBN 0 9520300 1 2
52 pages, 100 line illus, P/back
"Donald Grant has done it again ... in for a treat ... something here for all diabolo devotees ... enough to last a lifetime ... where will it all end?" The Catch.

ISBN 0 9520300 2 0
96 pages, 148 line illus, P/back
"An excellent and inspiring book ... everything is covered ... the usual humorous Grant style ... splendid illustrations ... a must for all aspiring diabolo experts ... a knowledgeable and expert teach-in." The Catch.

... and other authors.

ISBN 0 9520300 3 9
136 pages, 350 line illus, P/back
*"Probably the best single book on a juggling subject ... nicely written .. excellent illustrations." The Catch.
"... enough material here to last you a lifetime" Kaskade.*

ISBN 0 9520300 4 7
92 pages, 200 line illus, P/back
" About 76 years overdue ... user-friendly and supportive ... pass the Workshop Test? Answer: Yes, with flying colours ...tutorial feat." The Catch.

ISBN 0 9520300 6 3
72 pages, 95 line illus, P/back
" Not only fun to read but very clear." The Catch. "This is a real insider tip! ... all you need to turn a few tricks into a proper routine." Kaskade.

ISBN 0 9520300 7 1
76 pages, 120 line illus, A4 P/back
An immensely practical guide to the devilstick based on years of workshop experience